Salamanders

ABDO
Publishing Company

A Buddy Book
by
Julie Murray

VISIT US AT
www.abdopub.com

Published by Buddy Books, an imprint of ABDO Publishing Company, 4940 Viking Drive, Suite 622, Edina, Minnesota 55435. Copyright © 2005 by Abdo Consulting Group, Inc. International copyrights reserved in all countries. No part of this book may be reproduced in any form without written permission from the publisher.

Printed in the United States.

Edited by: Christy DeVillier
Contributing Editors: Matt Ray, Michael P. Goecke
Graphic Design: Maria Hosley
Image Research: Deborah Coldiron
Photographs: Corel, Mark Kostich, Jeff LeClere - www.herpnet.net, Minden Pictures, Dan Suizo

Library of Congress Cataloging-in-Publication Data

Murray, Julie, 1969-
  Salamanders/Julie Murray.
      p. cm. — (Animal Kingdom. Set II)
  Contents: Amphibians — Salamanders — Their bodies — Size and color — Where they live — What they eat — Senses — Defenses — Babies.
  ISBN 1-59197-334-1
    1. Salamanders—Juvenile literature. [1. Salamanders.] I. Title.

QL668.C2 M86 2003
597.8'5—dc21

2002038304

Contents

Salamanders Are Amphibians

The salamander's name means "lives in fire." Long ago, people thought salamanders had special powers. They thought salamanders could walk through fire and not get hurt. Today, people know this is not true.

Salamanders look like lizards. But they are not lizards. Salamanders are **amphibians**.

There are many kinds
of salamanders.

Amphibians have bare skin. They do not have feathers or hair. Amphibians spend part of their lives in water. They spend part of their lives on land, too. Other amphibians are frogs and toads.

Toads (below) and frogs (right) are amphibians, too.

Kinds Of Salamanders

Some salamanders live in the water most of their lives. This is true for mud puppies. Other salamanders live most of their lives on land. This is true for the slimy salamander. Some adult salamanders live on land and in the water. This is how the red-spotted newt lives.

The red-spotted newt lives in water and on land.

Size And Color

Salamanders can be many different sizes. The Chinese giant salamander is the longest **amphibian**. It grows to become almost five feet (two m) long. An adult pygmy salamander only grows about two inches (five cm) long.

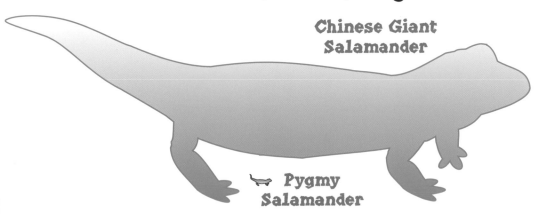

Chinese Giant
Salamander

Pygmy
Salamander

Five feet (Two meters)

Salamanders can be many colors. Many have spots or stripes. The northern red salamander is reddish orange with black spots. The marbled salamander is black, gray, and white. The California newt is dark on top with a brightly-colored belly.

Marbled salamander

Body Parts

Salamanders have a long tail. Most salamanders have four legs. Some only have two legs. Their feet have four or five toes. Salamanders do not have claws.

This salamander is shedding its skin.

Salamanders have wet skin. Many kinds of salamanders breathe air through their skin. Other salamanders use lungs for breathing. Mud puppies breathe with gills.

Mud puppy

Salamanders that live on land have moveable eyelids. They can close their eyes and blink. Salamanders that live in water do not have moveable eyelids.

Land salamander

Water salamander

Where They Live

Salamanders live in North America, South America, Europe, Africa, and Asia. Many of them live in cool, damp places. A good place to find salamanders is under rocks, leaves, or logs. Others live in trees or caves.

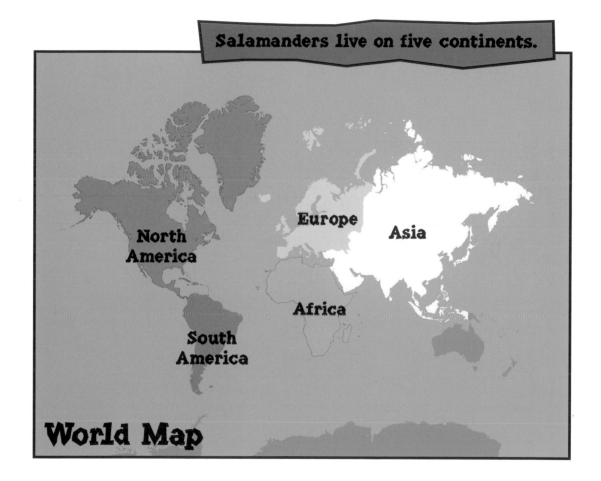

Salamanders live on five continents.

World Map

Europe

Asia

North
America

Africa

South
America

Hunting And Eating

Salamanders eat meat. They eat worms, insects, spiders, snails, and tadpoles. Larger salamanders also eat fish, mice, small snakes, and other salamanders.

A tiger salamander gets ready to catch a worm.

Salamanders hunt for food. Most use their sticky tongues to catch **prey**. Salamanders also have sharp teeth for holding prey. They swallow animals whole.

These salamanders are eating worms.

Guarding Against Predators

Salamanders must watch out for **predators**. Birds, snakes, fish, and other animals eat salamanders.

Some salamanders have colors that help them hide. Some salamanders have bright colors that warn predators to stay away. Other salamanders make poison in their skin.

A Salamander Trick

Many salamanders have another way of escaping **predators**. They drop their tail when a predator bites it. The predator often eats the fallen tail. This gives the salamander time to run away. It will grow a new tail over time.

Baby Salamanders

Female salamanders lay their eggs in different places. Some lay them in water. Others lay them on land. Many salamanders lay one or two eggs at a time. Some lay as many as 400 eggs at one time.

Salamander eggs

Baby salamanders born on land look like small adults. Baby salamanders born in water look very different. They have gills and no legs. These baby salamanders are called **larvae**.

Some **larvae** lose their gills. They grow lungs and legs. Then, they leave the water and live on land.

Other larvae keep their gills. They live their lives in the water. Salamanders can live for 30 years or more.

This salamander lives on land.

Important Words

amphibian   an animal that lives part of its life in water and part of its life on land.

larvae   a newborn amphibian.

predator   an animal that hunts and eats other animals.

prey   an animal that is food for other animals.

Web Sites

To learn more about salamanders, visit ABDO Publishing Company on the World Wide Web. Web sites about salamanders are featured on our Book Links page. These links are routinely monitored and updated to provide the most current information available.

www.abdopub.com

Index